I Can Do *That!*

A relational approach to sharing your faith.

Printed in the U.S.A.

Contents

A Relational Approach to Sharing Your Faith

Introduction 1-2-3

1 Winning the World begins with One

Value the __________________.

In the economy of God, lost people are infinitely valuable.

Luke 15 : The Lost Sheep

1 Now all the tax collectors and the
sinners were coming near Him to listen
to Him. 2 Both the Pharisees and the
scribes began to grumble, saying, "This
man receives sinners and eats with them."
3 So He told them this parable, saying,
4 "What man among you, if he has a hundred
sheep and has lost one of them, does not
leave the ninety-nine in the open pasture and
go after the one which is lost until he finds
it? 5 When he has found it, he lays it on his
shoulders, rejoicing. 6 And when he comes
home, he calls together his friends and his
neighbors, saying to them, 'Rejoice with me,
for I have found my sheep which was lost!'
7 I tell you that in the same way, there will
be more joy in heaven over one sinner who
repents than over ninety-nine righteous
persons who need no repentance.

The Lost Coin

8 Or what woman, if she has ten silver coins
and loses one coin, does not light a lamp and
sweep the house and search carefully until
she finds it? 9 When she has found it, she
calls together her friends and neighbors,
saying, 'Rejoice with me, for I have found
the coin which I had lost!' 10 In the same way,
I tell you, there is joy in the presence of the
angels of God over one sinner who repents.

Christians and non-Christians alike have something in common. We're both uncomfortable about evangelism.
—Rebecca Pippert

Psalm 56:3-4
When I am afraid, I will put my trust in you. In God, whose word I praise, in God have I put my trust; I shall not be afraid. What can mere man do to me?

2 Timothy 1:7-8
For God has not given us a spirit of timidity, but of power and love and discipline. Therefore, do not be ashamed of the testimony of our Lord, or of me His prisoner; but join with me in suffering for the gospel according to the power of God.

Fear Factors

Why aren't more Christians actively engaged in evangelism?

____

____

____

____

____

Options for Sharing Your Faith...

There are three major biblical models of evangelism: Proclamational, Confrontational (or Aggressive), and Relational. Each is demonstrated in the scriptures, and each has a culturally relevant representation today.

Model	*Passage*	*Biblical Example*	*Current Example*	*Requirements*	*Availability*
Proclamational Communicating the Gospel to a group, generally in public	Acts 2 Matthew 5	Peter Jesus	Billy Graham Most Churches	Natural Ability & Spiritual Gift	
Confrontational Communicating the Gospel to a person outside the context of an ongoing relationship	Acts 8 John 3	Phillip Jesus	Visitation Ministries	Personality & Spiritual Gift	
Relational Communicating the Gospel to a person in the context of an ongoing relationship	1 Thessalonians 2:7-11 John 1:14	Paul Jesus	Young Life Search	Friends	

2 Two Principles

1. Evangelism is a ______________.

The major decisions in life are the result of many mini-decisions.

John 4

[35] Do you not say, 'Four months more and then the harvest'? I tell you, open your eyes and look at the fields! They are ripe for harvest. [36] Even now the reaper draws his wages, even now he harvests the crop for eternal life, so that the sower and the reaper may be glad together. [37] Thus the saying 'One sows and another reaps' is true. [38] I sent you to reap what you have not worked for. Others have done the hard work, and you have reaped the benefits of their labor."

1 Corinthians 3

[5] What, after all, is Apollos? And what is Paul? Only servants, through whom you came to believe—as the Lord has assigned to each his task. [6] I planted the seed, Apollos watered it, but God made it grow. [7] So neither he who plants nor he who waters is anything, but only God, who makes things grow.

2. ___________ is responsible for the Results

When asked if she was frustrated by the fact that there were so many people she could not help, Mother Theresa responded, "No, for I am convinced that God does not expect me to be successful, but only faithful." We don't have to succeed, we just have to be faithful.

A *goal* is an objective under my control. A *desire* is an objective I may legitimately and fervently want, but I cannot reach it through my efforts alone. Dr. Larry Crabb, in *The Marriage Builder*.

Avoid Manipulation.

Differentiate between your Goals and Desires, then you can cultivate growing, non-manipulative relationships with people....

Pray for your desires.
Take responsibility for your goals.

Stages in the Process

A. TRUST CHRISTIAN — Can I trust you?

In our world, Christians are no longer given the benefit of the doubt. We are not well liked, we are often distrusted.
The first part of the process of evangelism is developing a trusting relationship with those that are far from Christ. This takes intentionality, compassion, patience, and desire. The easiest place to build relationships like this is around things that you enjoy. If you love golf, golf with non-Christians. If you love eating out, eat out with non-Christians.

Remember life events. Learn about their desires, hopes, dreams and struggles. Serve them and their family whenever you have a chance. Serve with them in their areas of interest.

Don't: Defend, Bruise, Avoid, Judge, Argue.
Do: Pray, Learn, Bond, Affirm, Welcome.

B. CURIOUS — Why do you act/think that way? Is there more to Jesus than I thought?

The second question that Christians should hope people will ask about them is, "Why do they act/think that way?" Why do they not let their emotions ride on success and failure in business, on athletic fields, and at home? Why do they remember my birthday each year? Why do they take the time to get to know all of the neighbors including the ones no one else likes? Was Jesus really like that?
Provoke Curiosity: Encourage questions, Use parables, Live curiosly, Don't douse curiosity by responding to a Dixie cup with a gallon of water.

C. CHANGE — The course I'm on may not be the best one. Perhaps I should change. Should I act/think your way?

Eventually, the Spirit of God needs to convict them of their sin, God's righteousness as displayed through our lives, and eventually his coming judgment. (John 16:8)
In order for this to happen we must continue to live lives that demand an explanation and we must learn to pay attention and ask good questions. Everyone has times in their life when they are more open to change. Often these occur in times when change is happening whether they like it or not; a new child is born, the loss of a loved one, their career changes, etc…

During these times we should learn to ask good questions. This stage often requires the most patience. Until a person is willing to change, all the right answers in the world won't move them closer to God.

Be patient as the Journey unfolds. Challenge as Jesus challenged. He touches the pain of the broken and honest, mobilized the self-pitying and fearful, connected the dots for the confused and befuddled. Practice Enduring Prayer. Use Soul-awakening events.

D. SEEKING — Is Jesus worth following? Am I willing to follow?

A person finally willing to change often still has questions about Jesus's worthiness. These people are true seekers, and need good, practical responses to their questions. Include them in your small groups, invite them to church, live out your Christian life in full view.

E. TRUST CHRIST — How do I begin a relationship with Christ?

At some point, we may need to gently urge them to place their faith in Christ. Can you do this clearly?

3 Three Barriers

Sharing your faith, (evangelism) is the process of making the Gospel clear. . . but there are often barriers in place that make the Gospel impossible to understand or embrace. Overcoming these barriers is an essential part of the process of evangelism.

There are 3 major barriers that keep people from embracing Christ.

E __________________ Barrier

I __________________ Barrier

V __________________ Barrier

The Emotional Barrier

Results from:

Their Response:

Our Responsibility:

1. Remember: Value the Person.

2. Develop ____________________ Based on Common Ground.

1 Corinthians 9:22 NLT
Yes, I try to find common ground with everyone so that I might bring them to Christ.

Common Ground: Definition

Areas of shared interest, background, experience, ability, or life situation that serve as the basis for developing and deepening a relationship.

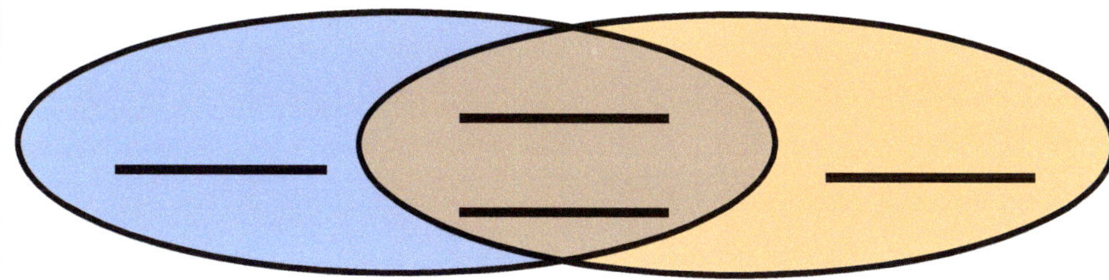

1 Corinthians 9 CSB

19 For although I am free from all people, I
have made myself a slave to all, in order ***to***
win more people. 20 To the Jews I became
like a Jew, ***to win*** Jews; to those under the
law, like one under the law—though I myself
am not under the law—***to win*** those under
the law. 21 To those who are outside the law,
like one outside the law—not being outside
God's law, but under the law of Christ—***to***
win those outside the law. 22 To the weak I
became weak, in order ***to win*** the weak. I
have become all things to all people, so that
I may by all means save some. 23 Now I do
all this because of the gospel, that I may
become a partner in its benefits.

Common Ground: Discovery

Develop the ____________________ of always looking for common ground.

Ask ____________________ with the intent of discovering another person's interests.

Once you have found common ground, __________________ the extent of it.

Make ___________________ to develop the relationship on common ground.

Your neighbors will have a hard time thinking you want them in heaven if you don't want them in your living room.

Limits of Common Ground

In 1 Corinthians 5:9-10 Paul clarifies his instructions not to associate with immoral people. In verse 10, he explicitly states, "I wasn't talking about unbelievers . . . .You would have to leave this world to avoid people like that."

Common Ground: Discernment

Common ground must never compromise

either your ____________ or your _____________.

3. Identify Your Network... the people in your communities

A person whose only friends are already committed to Christ can only share the Gospel with strangers. Your most natural opportunities for relationship development are the people in your network.

List the individuals within your network.

- You know them on a first name basis
- You have regular contact with them
- They don't seem to have a personal relationship with Christ
- You feel they are responsive to you, or would be open to cultivating a relationship based upon common ground.

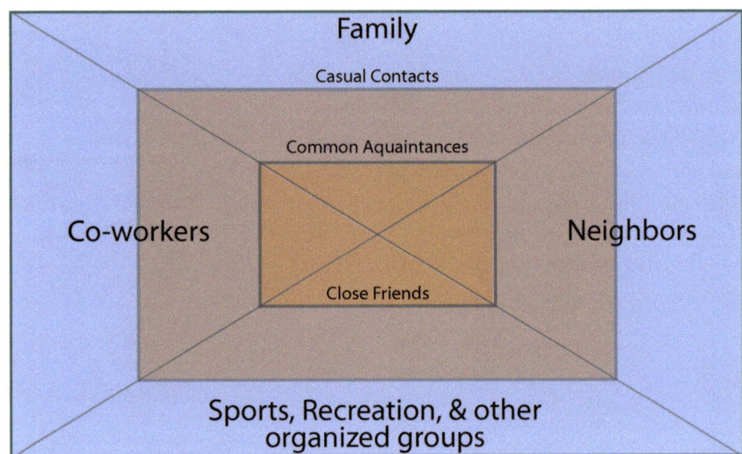

Name	Ways I can invest time with them next

Luke 16 *NIV*

Jesus told his disciples: "There was a rich
man whose manager was accused of wasting
his possessions. 2 So he called him in and
asked him, 'What is this I hear about you?
Give an account of your management,
because you cannot be manager any longer.'
3 "The manager said to himself, 'What shall
I do now? My master is taking away my
job. I'm not strong enough to dig, and I'm
ashamed to beg— 4 I know what I'll do so
that, when I lose my job here, people will
welcome me into their houses.'
5 "So he called in each one of his master's
debtors. He asked the first, 'How much do
you owe my master?'
6 "'Eight hundred gallons of olive oil.'
"The manager told him, 'Take your bill, sit
down quickly, and make it four hundred.'
7 "Then he asked the second, 'And how
much do you owe?'
"'A thousand bushels of wheat,' he replied.
"He told him, 'Take your bill and make it
eight hundred.'
8 "The master commended the dishonest
manager because he had acted shrewdly. For
the people of this world are more shrewd
in dealing with their own kind than are the
people of the light. 9 I tell you, use ***worldly***
wealth to gain friends for yourselves, so that
when it is gone, you will be welcomed into
eternal dwellings.

We take care of our health, we lay up money, we make our roof tight and our clothing sufficient, but who provides wisely that he shall not be wanting the best property of all—friends?

—Ralph Waldo Emerson

4. Invest for Eternity

The term used in this passage for worldly wealth is mammon – a derivative of an Aramaic term that is defined as wealth or property of any kind. Therefore when Jesus refers to mammon it has broad application including our treasure, our time, and our talents. The bottom line is one of stewardship. How are you doing in investing you time, talent, and treasures in the lives of your unchurched friends?

Invest your ____________________

Invest your ____________________

Invest your ____________________

Communication Skills

"Deepening Conversations"

Door #1 General Conversation

Check Doorknobs: Ask and share on the basic: name, family, occupation, where they live now, where they were raised, hobbies, sports, etc.
Keys: Ask questions. Listen
Goal: To establish common ground.
Pray that God would open doors to personal conversation.

Door #2 Personal Conversation

Check Doorknobs: Questions about their background. Questions and statements related to feelings. "That must have been a really frustrating time in your life." "You must have felt pretty low after that." "Would you say that was one of the difficult experiences in your life?"
Keys: Practice healthy self-disclosure. Listen
Goal: To establish trust.
Pray that God would open doors to spiritual conversations.

Door #3 Spiritual Conversation

Check Doorknobs: Sharing an element of your own religious background or personal testimony.
Questions related to religion, for example: "I guess I don't know much about your religious background. Were you raised in a religious home?"
Keys: Ask questions. Listen
Goal: To understand a person's spiritual interests and beliefs.
Pray that God would open doors to explain the Gospel.

Door #4 Gospel Presentation

Check Doorknobs: Transitional questions and statements, for example:
"Do you sense that you are moving toward a personal relationship with God? What would need to happen in your spiritual life for you to enter into a personal relationship with God ?"
"Have you come to a place in your own life where you know for certain that if you were to die today you would go to heaven? On a scale of one to ten, how sure are you?"
"Let's assume there is a God, a life after this life, and a heaven. If you were to die tonight and stand before God, and he were to say, "Why should I let you into heaven?" What would you say?"
Keys: Listen. Know a clear Gospel presentation and be ready to answer common objections.
Goal: To make the Gospel clear and give wise answers to key objections.
Pray that God would give them understanding and open a door for you to invite them to accept Christ.

Common Ground ideas for...

Organized Groups

What kinds of common ground activities do you feel you could comfortably and enjoyably participate in? Circle the areas of common ground listed below, or write out others.

Sports
Skiing
Golf
Cycling
Tennis
Hunting
Racquetball
Softball
Running
Basketball

Civic Clubs
Rotary Club
Kiwanis Club
Toastmasters
Lions Club
Salesmanship club
Jaycees
Neighborhood
Crime Watch
Gourmet Club
Taking walks
Local swim club
Gardening
Home Owners Association
Yard work

Volunteer Services
Fire
Junior League
Red Cross
Ambulance
Museum
Relief Efforts
Hospital
Symphony

Children's Activities
Boy Scouts
Little League
Model Railroading
4-H Club
Swim Team
Boys Club
P.T.A.
Toddler time / Mothers of Pre-Schoolers

Hobbies
Cooking
Board Games
Quilting
Antique Cars
Photography
Computer Users Groups
Woodworking
Painting

The Arts
Music
Symphony
Film
Theatre
Drama
Literature
Graphic arts

Other Ideas:

Common Ground ideas for...

Neighbors

These events should be designed toward building relationships without a Christian hook. This is not the time to slip in the gospel.

Relax, have fun and let the relationship grow. Trust the Lord for open doors for future harvesting. Check off some ideas in this list you find most helpful and make a note as to how you could apply them.

1. Have a party: a block, birthday, or seasonal party is an excellent relationship builder.
• Christmas: games, food, sharing family traditions. If small children are present, they could re-enact the Christmas story.
• Easter: food, games (egg hunt, egg relay, egg toss), time of brief sharing.
• Memorial Day: Invite everyone on the street. Get a high school or college couple to run games for the kids. Provide burgers, hot dogs, buns, and soft drinks. Assign even-numbered houses to bring salads & veggies, odd-numbered houses bring dessert.

2. Have a dinner: entertaining is a great way to build relationships.
• Progressive dinner: limit to a few families.
• Make it a Blockbuster night – with your neighbors. Pizza and a movie on a Friday night
• On a nice spring or fall evening, roll the grill out and invite the neighbors over for a spontaneous dinner in the backyard.
• During the summertime, plan a picnic at the park or lake with a family whose kids get along well with yours.

3. Be a good neighbor:
• Help rake leaves, shovel snow, trim hedges, or mow lawns.
• Be a lender. Be a borrower. Be a giver.
• Take dessert to a new neighbor. Remember birthdays, anniversaries.
• Take dinner to those a new mom, or a grieving family.

We don't think twice about helping out a fellow church member, the same kindness towards neighbors can go a long way towards building a trusting relationship.

Common Ground ideas for your

Co-workers

"When "ministry in the marketplace" is mentioned, it often sends a shudder down the spine of the working Christian. That's because "ministry in the marketplace" usually translates as "harvesting in the marketplace," which conjures up images of finding clever ways to present the entire gospel to each co-worker. Although the workplace can be a difficult place to harvest, it's an ideal place to sow."

—Tim Downs, Finding Common Ground

Workplace Guidelines: Use these guidelines as you prayerfully consider how you can more effectively witness while you work.

- ❑ Begin by looking at your job as one of the greatest opportunities you have to build redemptive relationships.
- ❑ Work hard to make your company and its people successful.
- ❑ Be committed to serving others in the company.
- ❑ Reflect a positive attitude in every aspect of your work.
- ❑ Make sure that anything labeled "Christian" with which you are involved is done with excellence.
- ❑ Pray for yourself and ask God to give you a heart for these people.
- ❑ Make a list of co-workers with whom you have the most contact and begin praying for them on a regular basis.
- ❑ Look for opportunities to spend social time together during the work day, at lunch, or on breaks.
- ❑ Look for ways you could further cultivate some of these relationships outside the workplace. Invite them to lunch, dinner, sporting events…
- ❑ Remember key dates and events in the lives of business associates: birthdays, anniversaries, weddings, illnesses, births. Send cards, call, and visit.
- ❑ Become active in your business athletic team(s).
- ❑ Join a local service club in the business community.
- ❑ Don't embarrass co-workers by your witness. Always be sensitive.
- ❑ Don't pressure anyone. Move toward those who seem interested.
- ❑ Don't try to make an impact for Christ alone. Identify other Christians in your workplace, and work together to reach out.
- ❑ Consider starting an investigative bible study for interested co-workers.
- ❑ Get training on building redemptive relationships. Talk to your pastor about the many valuable resources that are available.
- ❑ Study and apply the workplace strategy revealed in 1 Peter 2:12 and Colossians 3:23-25.

Adapted from *The Secular Bridge*, by Glenn Pate

The Intellectual Barrier

Results from:

Their Response:

Our Responsibility:

1. Prepare

1 Peter 3:15

▸ Learn to answer the 12 questions

** See pages 24-26 for more information on **I'm Glad You Asked**, the **Questions** workbook, and the **Search for Meaning** audio series.*

▸ Learn to present the Gospel clearly

1 Peter 3:15

15 But in your hearts set apart Christ as Lord. Always be prepared to give an answer to everyone who asks you to give the reason for the hope that you have. But do this with gentleness and respect.

Common Intellectual Objections

Do you know what you might say if asked one of these questions by a seeking friend?

Yes No

- ❑ ❑ Is there really a God?
- ❑ ❑ Why believe in miracles?
- ❑ ❑ Isn't religion just a crutch for weak-minded people?
- ❑ ❑ Is the Bible reliable?
- ❑ ❑ Why do the innocent suffer?
- ❑ ❑ Is Jesus Christ the only way to God?
- ❑ ❑ Will God judge those who have never heard of Christ?
- ❑ ❑ If Christianity is true, why are there hypocrites?
- ❑ ❑ Will my good works get me to heaven?
- ❑ ❑ Isn't salvation by faith too simple?
- ❑ ❑ What does the Bible mean by believe?
- ❑ ❑ Can anyone be sure of his salvation?

Colossians 4:4

4 Pray that I may proclaim it clearly, as I should.

Colossians 4:5-6
[5] Be wise in the way you act toward outsiders; make the most of every opportunity. [6] Let your conversation be always full of grace, seasoned with salt, so that you may know how to answer every one.

Proverbs 18:2, 13
[2] A fool finds no pleasure in understanding but delights in airing his own opinions.
[13] He who answers before listening—that is his folly and his shame.

James 1:19
My dear brothers, take note of this: Everyone should be quick to listen, slow to speak and slow to become angry.

The talk without the walk is hypocrisy. The walk without the talk is just a mystery.

2 Timothy 2:14, 24-26
[14]Keep reminding them of these things. Warn them before God against quarreling about words; it is of no value, and only ruins those who listen. [15] Do your best to present yourself to God as one approved, a workman who does not need to be ashamed and who correctly handles the word of truth … [23]
Don't have anything to do with foolish and stupid arguments, because you know they produce quarrels. [24] And the Lord's servant must not quarrel; instead, he must be kind to everyone, able to teach, patient when wronged. [25] Those who oppose him he must gently instruct, in the hope that God will grant them repentance leading them to a knowledge of the truth, [26] and that they will come to their senses and escape from the trap of the devil, who has taken them captive to do his will.

2. Walk the ________________

3. Talk the ________________

Listen with Love.

Raise the Issue.

Correct with Gentleness.

Communication Skills II

1. The Art of Listening

Real listening requires focused attention. It involves:

- Taking genuine interest rather than planning your next move.
- Communicating acceptance rather than passing judgment before the other person is finished.
- Being patient rather than trying to close the conversation as quickly as possible.
- Being courteous rather than repeatedly interrupting and fighting for the floor.
- Valuing another's ideas rather than missing what he means and feels.

The way we listen will communicate whether we regard the other person as important. "He who has, ears to hear, let him hear" (Matt. 11:15).

How do we put this into practice?

Here are six suggestions:

1. Listen for the expression of interests in the areas of personal background, family, vocation, recreation, and culture. This is the key to friendship, because you are looking for areas of common ground.
2. Listen for the expression of felt needs. What is this person willing to admit about himself? This is the key to opportunities to tell about the only one who can meet our needs.
3. Listen for the expression of previous or present religious experience, without pressure or condescension. This is the key to appreciating another's position.
4. Listen for the expression of caricatures of Christianity. This is the key to overcoming obstacles.
5. Ask clarifying and probing questions. This is the key to understanding.
6. Ask inquiring, provocative, and challenging questions. This is the key to helping people think their way to Christ.

2. Responses that *Stimulate*

Here are some principles for participating in a discussion that will increase openness and decrease defensiveness.

1. ***When stating your position, you can preface your remarks with tentative statements.*** You may be absolutely sure of your position. But when you preface a remark with a tentative statement, it promotes an atmosphere of openness and enhances the quality of the discussion.
   - I understand what you're saying, but let me tell you how I see it.
   - I'm just wondering, have you ever considered this _______?
   - In my opinion…
   - How would you respond to this: _______?
   - Have you considered the evidence for ________?
   - Can I give you another option?
2. ***When you want another person in the group to say more you can respond this way:***
   - I'm not sure I understand what you're saying, tell me more.
   - Is this what you're saying __________?
   - What do you mean by the term __________?
   - Can you explain (or illustrate) that?
   - How are you defining __________?
   - I'm not sure I see where the conflict is.
   - So essentially what you're saying is, __________.
   - It seems like you're saying, __________.
   - I understand what you are getting at. You're saying __________.
3. ***When you want to express your disagreement...***
   - What you're saying raises some red flags in my mind.
   - My perception of this issue is a little different. Can I share it with you?
   - I'm not piecing together the facts in the same way.
   - Correct me if I'm wrong, but I see a conflict between - and
   - That would make a lot of sense to me, but
   - This doesn't seem to fit with what you've said before.
   - I appreciate that perspective. However, let me tell you how I view it.
4. ***When you agree...***
   - That's really good. I've never heard it put that way before.
5. ***When you partially agree...***
   - I agree with you (state what you agree with) but I'm not seeing eye-to-eye on this other issue.
6. ***When you want to stimulate discussion...***
   - Wait. I'd be interested in _________'s reaction to that…
   - How does what you're saying relate to this comment?

3. Reactions that *Stifle*

Beware of these responses. When someone forcefully expresses a view that belittles or puts down your faith, emotions soar and it is easy to respond with these kinds of statements.

Here are the discussion stiflers:

- It's a proven fact that...
- That's just the way it is...
- There's no question about...
- Only fools believe...
- (Using a dogmatic tone of voice) The Bible says...
- You don't know what you're talking about...
- That's ridiculous...
- Look at the evidence...
- That just doesn't fit the facts...
- You're not serious...
- Well, if you believe that, then...
- There's just no evidence for...
- That's been totally disproved...
- Any reasonable person can see...
- Give me a break, that was refuted years ago...
- That's a self-defeating argument; you've just said something that's impossible.
- You're being totally illogical.
- How can you even say that?
- They say...

How to Transition *from Small Talk... to Spiritual Things*

Here are five ways you can "make the most of the opportunity" and "know how you should respond to each person." (Colossians 4:5, 6)

Step One: Determine their readiness

To effectively move a discussion from small talk to spiritual things you first need to determine your friend's readiness.

- ❑ What do you know of the person's religious background?
- ❑ What opportunities have you had to "plant seeds"? What was the response?
- ❑ Do you sense that your neighbor enjoys being with you?
- ❑ What needs have you discovered that relate to the gospel solution?
- ❑ What caricatures have you been able to eliminate from his arsenal of questions and excuses?
- ❑ How much of your personal testimony have you had a chance to share? How has he or she responded?

Four signs that a person may be open to a discussion about the gospel message:

- ❑ They ask questions.
- ❑ They are willing to read books that answer their questions.
- ❑ They are willing to explore reasons for belief.
- ❑ They seem free from a defensive attitude when discussing spiritual issues.

Step Two: Learn a few transitions

Here are five transitional questions and statements that will help you move into conversations about spiritual things.

The "Why should I let you in?" Question

"Let's assume there is a God, a life after this life, and a heaven. If you were to die tonight and stand before God, and he were to ask you 'Why should I let you into my heaven?' What would you say?"

The Assurance Question

"Have you come to the place in your spiritual life where you know for certain that if you were to die today you would go to heaven? On a scale of 1-10 how sure are you?"

The Spiritual Pilgrimage Questions

"John, we've never talked much about your religious background. I'm curious, where are you in your spiritual pilgrimage (or spiritual pursuits)?"

"Do you sense that you are moving toward a personal relationship with God? Would you like to know how to enter into a personal relationship with God?"

"If a relationship with God were possible, what do you think it would be like?"

Step Three: Set up the opportunity

Here are a few ideas for setting up the time to talk with a friend about entering into a personal relationship with God.

Use an opportunity statement.

"Sometime I'd like the opportunity to share some principles that have helped me understand what it means to establish a personal relationship with Christ."

Try to spark an interest.

"Sometime I'd love to share those principles with you"

Find a time.

"When would be a good time? Could we get together for breakfast or lunch?"

"Why don't we play tennis together and we can discuss the principles after the game."

Step Four: Share the message.

For an example of comfortably sharing the message, we recommend you listen to Dialogues 9-12 in The Search for Meaning audio series.

Ask for an opportunity to explain the message.

When you sense you have an opportunity to communicate the essence of the gospel message, the following questions are very helpful.

- ❑ *"Would you be interested in seeing what the Bible says about how you can know for sure that you have eternal life?"*
- ❑ *"Would you be interested in seeing what the Bible says about how you can enter into a personal relationship with God?"*
- ❑ *"Has anyone ever shown you how you can experience God's love and forgiveness? May I?"*

After you've finished presenting the message of the gospel, these two questions will help move a person either toward belief, or toward more exploration of how the gospel meets his or her ultimate need for a relationship with God.

Discern their readiness to make a decision.

"On the basis of this information do you feel you have ever received Jesus Christ as your savior? Do you feel you are ready o take this step?"

Follow up with questions.

"I understand that this is a new concept and that it takes a while to digest it before you make a decision. Would you be interested in meeting once a week for three weeks and going through a study on what it means to start a relationship with God?"

Gather and remember good illustrations.

You will find many useful illustrations in resources like *I'm Glad You Asked,* and *The Search for Meaning* audio series. Current events and periodicals offer many examples of man's quest for meaning. Illustrations are one of the most effective means of communicating a message.

Step Five: Avoid the Pitfalls.

When you communicate the message of the gospel, avoid these common mistakes.

- ❑ Don't use cliché's or theological language.
  Practice the presentation using creative alternatives to the traditional words.
- ❑ Don't do all the talking.
  Ask questions as you move through the presentation – make sure they are still with you.
- ❑ Don't come across as dogmatic or authoritarian.
  Work at being sensitive and understanding toward the world view of others.
- ❑ Don't force the issue.
  Asking a person t believe may not be appropriate on every occasion. Be sensitive to the other person and to the leading of the Holy Spirit.

Consider this...

Whether it is movies, religion, politics, current events, or food, your friends will tell you about issues and experiences that are important to them, and they don't expect you to always agree with them. These discussions can provide natural opportunities to discuss spiritual topics. If you work at relationships, you should feel free to share your faith without the fear of losing your friend.

The Volitional Barrier

Results from:

Their Response:

Our Responsibility:

1. Understand their ________________.

They are ____________________.

They are ____________________.

They are ____________________.

Ephesians 2:1-2
[1] As for you, you were dead in your
transgressions and sins, [2] in which you used
to live when you followed the ways of this
world and of the ruler of the kingdom of the
air, the spirit who is now at work in those
who are disobedient.

2 Corinthians 4:3-4
[3] And even if our gospel is veiled, it is veiled
to those who are perishing. [4] The god of this
age has blinded the minds of unbelievers, so
that they cannot see the light of the gospel of
the glory of Christ, who is the image of God.

2 Timothy 2:24-26
[24] And the Lord's servant must not quarrel;
instead, he must be kind to everyone, able to
teach, patient when wronged. [25] Those who
oppose him he must gently instruct, in the
hope that God will grant them repentance
leading them to a knowledge of the truth, [26]
and that they will come to their senses and
escape from the trap of the devil, who has
taken them captive to do his will.

*The unbeliever is not the enemy;
he is the victim of the enemy.*

Acts 4:29-31
[29] Now, Lord, consider their threats and enable your servants to speak your word with great boldness. [30] Stretch out your hand to heal and perform miraculous signs and wonders through the name of your holy servant Jesus."
[31] After they prayed, the place where they were meeting was shaken. And they were all filled with the Holy Spirit and spoke the word of God boldly.

Ephesians 6:18-19
[18] And pray in the Spirit on all occasions with all kinds of prayers and requests. With this in mind, be alert and always keep on praying for all the saints.
[19] Pray also for me, that whenever I open my mouth, words may be given me so that I will fearlessly make known the mystery of the gospel,

Colossians 4:2-4
[2] Devote yourselves to prayer, being watchful and thankful. [3] And pray for us, too, that God may open a door for our message, so that we may proclaim the mystery of Christ, for which I am in chains. [4] Pray that I may proclaim it clearly, as I should.

Romans 10:1
Brethren, my heart's desire and my prayer to God for them is for their salvation

Zechariah 4:6
Not by might, nor by power, but by my Spirit, says the Lord God Almighty.

Philippians 4:13
I can do everything through him who gives me strength.

Acts 1:8
"But you will receive power when the Holy Spirit comes on you; and you will be my witnesses in Jerusalem, and in all Judea and Samaria, and to the ends of the earth."

Acts 1:14
These all with one mind were continually devoted to prayer

Talk to God about people before you talk to people about God. To pray is to declare our dependence on God, to not pray is to declare our independence from Him.

2. Rely on God's ____________________ .

3. Pray with ____________________ .

How?

For What?

For Whom?

Group Exercise: Prayer

Review

Begin with 1

Winning the world begins with _______.
Luke 15:7

Value each _______________.

2 Principles

Evangelism is a _______________.
John 4:34-38

God is responsible for the _______________.
1 Corinthians 3:5-7

3 Barriers

The Emotional Barrier

My Focus... _______________.
1 Corinthians 9:19-23

The Intellectual Barrier

My Focus... _______________.
1 Peter 3:15

The Volitional Barrier

My Focus... _______________.
Colossians 4:2-6

Proceed to Discipleship...

Do not be satisfied to be merely active; you can be active but not necessarily productive. Neither satisfy yourself with being merely productive. We are called to be reproductive. Not only are we to lead people to Christ, we are to disciple them so they can lead others to Christ, and so on.

2 Timothy 2:1-2
You, therefore, my son, be strong in the grace that is in Christ Jesus. And the things which you have heard from me in the presence of many witnesses, these entrust to faithful men, who will be able to teach others also.

The Four Generations of 2 Timothy 2:2

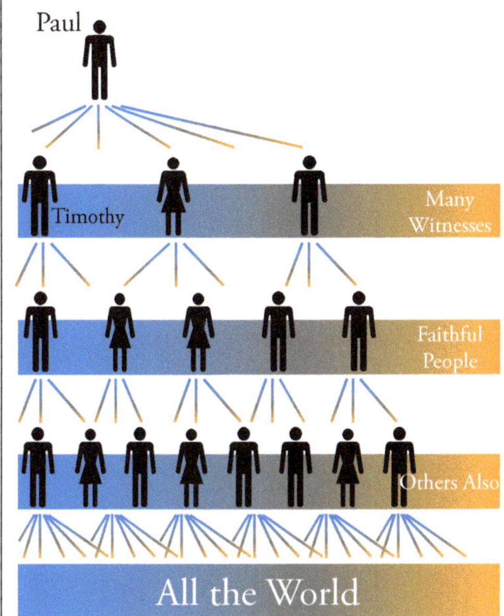

Street Level Apologetics

Search's Resources

I'm Glad You Asked:

This is Search's original apologetics resource, written to help Christians answer the tough questions most people ask about Christianity—questions such as: How can there be a good God with all the suffering in the world? or Isn't religion just another psychological crutch? The text guides you logically through these questions with helpful flow charts and practical illustrations. It shows how each objection is really an opportunity to explain the Gospel. *I'm Glad You Asked* is yet another tool for building the faith of the believer, as well as equipping you to personally answer the questions your seeking friends ask.

Second Option: Christianity is Objective

If the Resurrection of Jesus is true, so is Christianity.

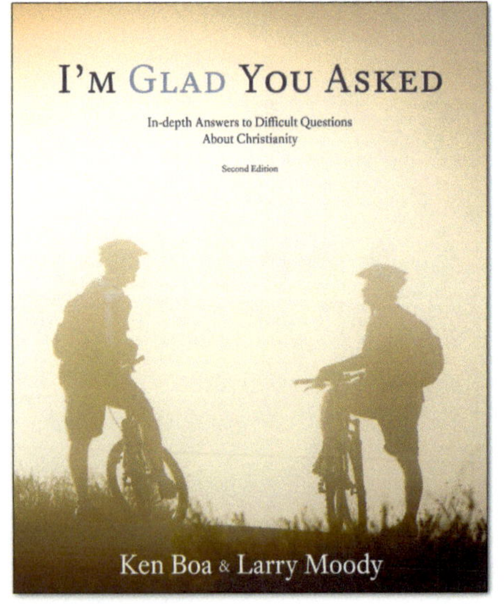

QUESTION 4: IS THE BIBLE RELIABLE?

Often Asked Questions:

- The Bible has been copied and translated so many times—hasn't this process led to errors?
- How can you be sure that the Bible is the same now as when it was written?
- Is there any proof from archaeology that the stories in the Bible happened?
- Is it true that most of the books of the Bible were not written by the people whose names are put on them as authors?
- Isn't the Bible full of contradictions and errors?
- Doesn't the Bible make a number of claims that are scientifically inaccurate?
- Didn't the church arbitrarily decide which books should be included in the Bible and which books should be rejected?
- How can you place your faith in a book that condones genocide and slavery?
- So many people have different interpretations of the Bible—what makes you think that yours is correct?

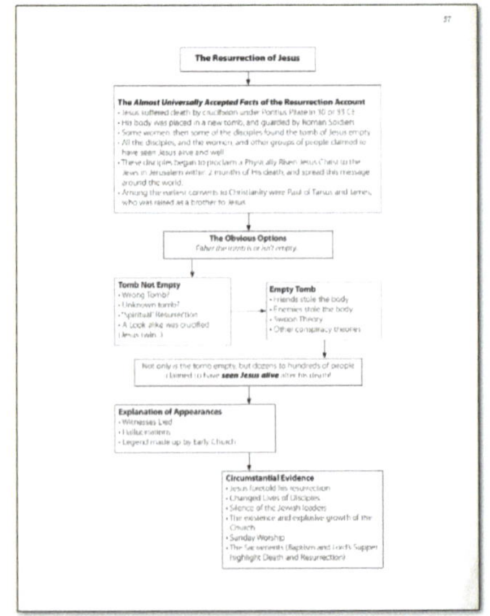

The Search For Meaning Audio Series:

This **6-CD set** is comprised of twelve conversations between a seeker and a Christian about the typical questions that a friend evaluating Christianity is likely to ask. These low key, yet informative conversations were designed for Christians as training and for those still seeking the truth.

The Search For Answers:

This **CD** takes the 25 minute discussion s of The Search For Meaning and boils them down into preliminary five-minute responses. Here you will find brief discussions which include real evidence and logical responses, not simply dogma, emotionalism or a leap of faith. Honest seekers and doubters who want faith in God to make sense will find real help in these dialogues, as will those who desire to give reasons for their faith.

DIALOGUE #9 – How good must we be to qualify for heaven?

Lamar: Well, Bill, what did you think about the training seminar? I kept thinking I'd run into you in the hotel lobby some time this week, but they kept us so busy!

Bill: Yeah, I feel like I need a vacation now. I don't know why they sent us to these nice locations and then schedule meetings from early in the morning to late in the afternoon. As far as the seminar, I thought it was well above average with lots of useful information. And I actually think it was pretty worthwhile. What'd you think?

Lamar: Well, I'm, I'm not so sure that what's best about these things isn't simply the opportunity to get away from the rat race long enough to think a little, to kind of sort things out, to ask some good questions, and to be asked some good questions that are thought provoking. You know, have a chance to get a fresh perspective.

Bill: You mean having time to sharpen the ax?

Lamar: Exactly! I feel like I've been swinging with a dull ax and that I really can't take the time out to sharpen it. Then I get out of town for training and I realize all over again that I really can't afford not to take the time out to sharpen it.

Bill: Great point, Lamar. Now that I think about it, I could get a lot of the same benefit at home if I took out the time to do more reflecting.

Lamar: I quite agree. That's my experience. That's one of the reasons I value so highly the talks that you and I have been having about God. These talks have allowed me to sharpen the ax, so to speak, in maybe the most important area of all.

Bill: That reminds me, I was about to ask you a question at the end of our discussion on hypocrisy right before they served our meal, then I fell asleep after dinner.

Lamar: Yeah, you were really out. You'd been pushing it pretty hard the previous two weeks, as I recall, and I didn't really have the heart to wake you up. Do you still remember the question?

Bill: Yes, I do as a matter of fact. It's just hypothetical, but it's one of those great cut-through-the-smoke type of questions. Hear it is. If you were standing at the gate of Heaven and God asked you, "Lamar, why should I let you into my Heaven?" What would you say?

Lamar: You mean if this plane goes down this afternoon and I am face to face with my maker, what would I say to him?

Bill: Yep, that's the question! What would your answer be?

Lamar: Well, um, hmm, I guess I'd say that while I'm not sure I stack up too well against the lives of some of the people you were describing on the flight up here, you know, the sincere, non-hypocrites, I think I've tried to live my life according to the "golden rule" and, for that matter, the ten commandants. I'm committed to being a good husband and father and to treating people the way I'd like to be treated. Um, that really is a good question and, uh, I guess I'm not completely comfortable with my answer, Bill. Uh, let me, let me ask you, what would you say to that question?

Bill: Well, if I answered God by saying that I should be let in because I've led a good life, I'm convinced that I'd flunk. That he wouldn't let me in.

Lamar: What now? Why do you think you wouldn't make it?

Bill: Because, it seems that the more I learn about God and about what he expects, the more I learn about what real goodness is on the one hand, and on the other hand, the more honest I'm willing to be about myself, the more impressed I become about how terribly far short I fall, how unqualified I am to earn a spot in Heaven.

Lamar: Bill, what on earth are you talking about? I've always thought of you as one of the really good guys and I've always looked up to you. Were you a serial killer before I met you?

Disc 5 Track : 2

The goodness and justice of God (6:44)

Bill: No, it's, it's just that Jesus defined goodness much differently than we do. Early in the Sermon on the Mount, before he gave the golden rule, he said, "Therefore, you are to be perfect, as your heavenly father is perfect." And before that, he told the people that unless their goodness was better than the goodness of the religious leaders, they wouldn't make it into the kingdom of Heaven. Then he went on and explained why the religious leaders, do-gooders that they were, didn't qualify.

Lamar: Okay, were these the ones you were talking about who got upset because Jesus called them, um, hypocrites?

Bill: Yes, the same ones. Jesus said it's not only wrong to commit murder, but that it is wrong to curse your brother or to harbor a grudge. Not only wrong to commit adultery, but wrong to allow yourself to think lustful thoughts.

Lamar: Ah ha, that's Jimmy Carter.

Bill: That's where he's quoting from, exactly. In other words, it's not only a sin to commit a wrong act; it's a sin to have the wrong thoughts and attitudes. The idea is that God not only cares about what we do on the outside that others can see, but about what's on the inside of us that no one else may know about. His standard is perfection, not some dumbed down moral mediocrity.

Lamar: Wait a minute, Bill. That, that sounds impossible. Surely God can't really expect perfection. I thought you believed in a God of love and forgiveness?

Bill: I do, but I don't want to fall prey to the peril of the pendulum.

Lamar: The peril of the pendulum? What's that supposed to be?

Bill: Well, you know how a pendulum works. It swings from one extreme to the other, but never stops in the middle and that's the way it seems like it is with popular notions about God. One extreme is to think of God as some heavenly ogre or ....spewing out hellfire and damnation and brimstone, or it's as if he were booming a question out from Heaven, "Is anyone down there having a good time?" Somebody says yes and God shouts back, "Well, cut it out!"

Lamar: Well, yeah, frankly growing up in a very rural and very Southern state, that's exactly the kind of God that I learned about from as early as I can remember. Don't, don't, don't! Anything that was fun was sinful by definition. We were constantly reminded of what awful sinners we were and even with a bony finger pointed at us at times from the pulpit. And if we weren't saved, whatever that meant, we'd fry in torment in hell forever. Shame, guilt, and fear were the main motivators. I thought they taught it at seminary.

Bill: Although you'd probably think your church was unique in this, that conception of God was fairly common. It's a terrible distortion and slander against the God of the Bible and it causes a lot of damage. But you know there's another equally great error to be avoided on the opposite swing of the pendulum?

Lamar: Which is?

Bill: The idea that God is only a God of love. That love is the only divine characteristic of any importance and that holiness, purity, justice, and truth really don't matter. God, for many people, even for a lot of ministers, is like some senile, old grandfather in the sky who hears no evil and sees no evil. C.S. Lewis said that some people's concept of God is that his only concern is that it could be said at the end of the day that a good time was had by all. Is everybody having fun?

Lamar: You know, I hate to ask a dumb question, but what's the matter with that?

Bill: Well, first of all, it leaves evil unpunished. Secondly, if God's not just and holy, as well as loving, then I submit he's not even loving.

Lamar: How's that?

Bill: Well, imagine yourself as a Jew in the Holocaust with scars both physically and emotionally, uh, your family's been tortured and killed. If God doesn't plan to deal out justice to Hitler and his cohorts, not in this life, not in the next, would you feel like he loves you?

Lamar: If he knew that someone was torturing me and he never planned to bring him to justice?

Bill: Never.

Lamar: I would feel very much abandoned and unloved.

Bill: Take away justice and you end up taking away love. It's his love that motivates him to bring justice to those who use the free will he lovingly gave them to harm other creatures he loves. Let me try another example.

Lamar: Good, cause, uh, I'm still struggling with this necessity for God to have the perfect standard and to judge people. Isn't that what being sorry and asking forgiveness is all about?

Bill: Nope, different issue! Now, imagine that I'm short on cash... [Dialogue Continues...]

Useful Illustrations

3 Illustrations on the relationship between Love & Justice

LaGuardia Justice & Love can exist together During the Great Depression, police brought an elderly man before a New York City night court magistrate. The man was starving and had stolen a loaf of bread.

That night Mayor Fiorello LaGuardia was presiding over the court, as he sometimes did to stay close to the citizens. He fined the old man $10. The law is the law, and cannot be broken, The mayor said. At the same time, he took a $10 dollar bill out of his wallet and paid the fine for the old man.

Then LaGuardia cited each person in the courtroom for living in a city that did not help its poor and elderly, unduly tempting them to steal. The mayor fined everyone in the courtroom 50 cents and gave almost $50 to the amazed defendant. Both justice and love were served when LaGuardia paid the penalty and more for the elderly man.

Sorry Criminal (SFM Dialogue 9) We yearn for justice Imagine that Im short on cash and I decide to rob a convenience store. In the midst of the robbery my mask falls off and knowing that he might identify me, I impulsively shoot and kill the clerk.

But as I read about the grieving widow and her four children, my remorse and guilt overwhelm me until I finally turn myself into the authorities and plead guilty at the trial. After Im pronounced guilty and it is time for sentencing, lets imagine that I approach the bench and that youre the judge. Your honor, Im terribly sorry for what I have done. I want to do better with my life and I ask you for a pardon. Will you let me go free?

Even if you are able to somehow supernaturally see inside me and know that I was truly sorry, and you could see into the future and know that Id never commit that crime again. Will you let me go?

Suppose the widow and children arent screaming for revenge. Theyre simply numb with pain over their irretrievable loss. Now will you let me go?

Something just doesnt seem right about letting me go scot-free. Not because were mean and vengeful, its because were caring and because we have a sense of justice. The fact that Im sincerely sorry doesnt remove the need for justice.

To show that love without justice is impossible God is a loving God, so He wont judge those who have not heard of or responded to Him

I tell you that I love my wife and kids. I say that I could talk for hours about how much I love them. When I get home tonight, I discover that theyve been involved in a terrible hit and run accident with a reckless/drunk driver. My son dies and my wife is paralyzed. The next week I discover the identity of the reckless/drunk driver and say, Im sure he didnt mean anything by it, well just let it go this time. The next time you and I talk and I tell you how much I love my family, do you believe me? No, in fact you might wonder whether I had hired the guy to take out my family. If I am not crying out for justice, then you have every right to doubt the love I claim for my family. Justice without love is cruel. Love without justice is not love at all.

God loves me too much not to impose justice on those who have hurt me. God loves those that Ive hurt too much to allow me to escape justice.

Other useful illustrations

Hikers & Icy Lake To illustrate: Faith is only as valid as the object in which it is placed Two men are hiking in Colorado in January. When dusk came upon them quickly, their only hope for getting back to the lodge before dark was to cut across the lake. One of the men was afraid that the ice would not support him and hesitated. His experienced friend reminded him that it was the middle of January, the ice had to be at least six feet thick, and they had no reason to worry. The frightened man had little faith and so he inched his way back to the lodge. The ice supported him; his faith was small but its object was strong. Later that year the two men were again hiking and dusk came upon them suddenly. The once fearful man now suggested they cut across the lake. The first man, however, told his now brave friend that it was now late May and the ice was no thicker than a quarter of an inch. But he could not be dissuaded, for his faith was great. So he ventured a few feet from shore and crashed through the ice. His faith was much stronger the second time, but the object of his faith far less sound. Our faith is only as good as its object. Restated, the validity of the object is more important than the strength of the faith.

BIBLE - Telephone Game -Hasnt the bible been drastically changed over the years? Everyone remembers the telephone game from childhood. One boy whispers a phrase to the girl sitting next to him, and the message is whispered around the circle. The last person says aloud what he thinks the message is, often with hilarious results. Through many transmissions, the message has become grossly distorted. The process of copying the Bible has been compared to this game. But in order to make the comparison fair, we would have to make this adjustment. The first person would say the message out loud to the person sitting next to him and the message would be repeated out loud around the entire circle. If someone deliberately changed the messaged or got it wrong on accident, anyone who caught the mistake would be able to correct them. The Bible was not copied in secret or through hushed voices, but was conducted openly.

BIBLE - JFK Witnesses Didnt the writers of the New Testament just make up stories about Jesus? Suppose a man wrote a book today claiming that after he was shot in Dallas, John F. Kennedy came back to life, appeared to groups of people around the country for a couple of weeks and then disappeared. How many copies would he sell? Probably quite a few. But could this new view gather a large following? Probably not. There are simply too many eye witnesses to the events of 1963 still alive today to contradict this fiction. The book might garner a few headlines, but it would only be months before its believers could be found only in the fringes of society. And yet the stories of Christs death and resurrection were circulated immediately in the very place where he died and the first gospels were written down within 30 years.

BIBLE - Interview Facts Suppose I interviewed you about your grandmother. We spent the afternoon together as you recount her history, her education, when she got married, the births of your aunts and uncles, her community services, and many other anecdotes. How do I know what youve told me is true? If I looked up public records, i.e. birth records, marriage certificates, transcripts, and you got a few of the details wrong, I might have reason to doubt some of the other stories that you spun for me - you are not a reliable historian. But if your story agreed with the public records, and I was able to corroborate a few other events with other sources, like newspaper articles or mutual acquaintances, then I would come to see you as a reliable witness to your grandmothers life, and ascribe a measure of credibility to the rest of the stories. The Bible records many conversations, and events that cannot be independently verified. No Roman historian bothered to record the outcome of a sisterly spat between Mary and Martha over kitchen duties. But the writers of scripture recorded numerous details about the times in which the events took place. They did not know what we could or could not check up on two thousand years later. And yet, every time the Bible and archeology overlap they agree. If the authors of scripture were so careful in recording historical details that we can check up on, what should we assume about the details we cant check? Archaeology cant prove the bible, but its corroboration with biblical details gives tremendous credibility to the historicity of scripture.

Another Look at Hell Imagine being around somebody who was better looking, more intelligent, a better conversationalist, more athletic, more creative, and wealthier than you. This person exceeds all of your strengths, and excels in your areas of weakness. In social situations, if this person is present, you are ignored. In fact you are irrelevant in every situation where the two of you show up together. No one, in any scenario, would choose you over this person. Now imagine being handcuffed to this person for the rest of your life. What would this be like? Depressing, painful, torturous you can think of others. Only one scenario could make this situation tolerableif you, yourself, were head over heels in love with this person. If you were so thrilled just to be with this person that you didnt care who paid attention to you. Actually, you would rather talk about this person than yourself. One way or the other, this would be life in eternity with the God, with Jesus. He possesses unspeakable beauty, infinite intelligence, absolute integrity, and any other superlative you can think of. For those who have learned to love him, to value the things he values, to be with him will be a wonderful, joyous, ecstaticit would be Heaven. But to force people who dont love him to spend eternity in his presence, doing the things that people who love him would want to do, would be cruel indeed. Instead of imposing this never-ending torture on people who would rather not be with him, out of his mercy he created a place where he was notHell. It is a place for people who would not want to go to Heaven.

Who determines truth? If an individual can declare truth, then there is no room to criticize Charles Manson or Ted Bundy. They just acted according to what was true for them. If a societal group can determine truth for itself, then we have no room to criticize the actions of inner city gangs or the Ku Klux Klan. They simply acted according to what they had determined to be truth. If truth can be determined by larger groups, like nations and kingdoms, then we have no room to criticize Hitlers Germany, Europes crusades, or Stalins USSR. Only if truth is an objective standard outside of people, groups, or nations can we rightfully condemn the horrific actions of these people and regimes.

Unleaded Gas (IGYA p157) Suppose someone feels that the auto makers are cramping his style by specifying unleaded gas only for his automobile. If he resisted this narrow confine by using diesel fuel or, worse yet, water, his car would cease to operate. The specifications may be narrow, but nevertheless they are valid. what he wants to believe, and to treat him with dignity because he is made in the image of God. But I cannot say that his beliefs are true, or even have merit.

Travel Directions to illustrate the Law of Non-contradiction If I say that one can get from Baltimore** to Washington by driving on Interstate 95, and you say that one can get to the same place by taking 295 or 70 and 29, we might both be right. But if I say that the ONLY way to get from Baltimore to Washington is on Interstate 95, and you say, There is another way, on 295, Then we have a contradiction. Either one of us could be right, or we could both be wrong. But we cannot both be correct. **Use cites and roads nearby Every religion claims to be the only way to gain the most from the afterlife. They may all be wrong, but they cannot all be right.

Airplane faith is only as good as the object in which it is placed Every time you get on an airplane, you put faith in the plane and the pilot. Trusting that the plane is well made and the pilot is well trained, you believe that you will arrive safely at your destination within a matter of hours. Millions of these acts of faith take place every day around the world. 99.999% of the time the faith is well-placed. The objects of their faith the plane and the pilot get the passengers safely to their destination. Sometimes their faith is misplaced. Either the pilot or the plane was not up to the task. The object of the passengers faith failed, and the faith was useless. Faith is only as good as the object in which it is placed.

Aids Illustration My good works are not the issue Three men are dying of AIDS. One contracted the HIV virus through promiscuous sexual activity, another a lifelong heroin addict got it though a dirty needle. The third man, a hemophiliac, was infected by a transfusion with contaminated blood. Two of the individuals were involved in illicit or illegal activities, but all three face the same prognosis an untimely demise to an incurable disease.

They are all taking AZT to treat the symptoms. Although not a cure, AZT slows the effects of the virus, prolonging and enhancing the life of an AIDS victim.

Today the cure for AIDS is discovered, a completely different compound: TZA. While this new compound appears to cure AIDS, it has disastrous effects if combined with AZT - patients must choose one or the other.

The hemophiliac has attained a pretty normal life with AZT, so he continues his normal treatments. The druggie resolves to clean up his life. He kicks his habit, gets a job, and starts taking care of himself in addition to the AZT treatments. The gigolo accepts the offer to take TZA.

This promiscuous man is cured. The other two men, in spite of their good lives and best efforts, will still die from the complications of AIDS someday.

All systems of Good Works operate like spiritual AZT - almost any system of good works prolongs and enhances this life. Where do good works fit into peoples eternal destiny?

They dont. Just like AZT, they provide a better life, but fail to change the eventual outcome. We all have an incurable disease called sin. No amount of getting better will let us reach sinless. No amount of future good can undo the damage already done. We dont need a spiritual crutch, we need a cure.

Hypocrites - Robbing a 7-11

Joe walks into the 7-11 with a ski mask on and gun in the air. As he instructs the clerk to empty the cash drawer, he announces that he is under orders from Peter not to leave any witnesses. When the drawer is empty, Joe unloads two bullets into the clerk and makes his getaway.

The police arrive moments later and find the clerk on the floor covered in blood and gasping for air.

Can you give a description of your assailant? The officer asks.

With his final breaths, the clerk weakly replies, All I know is that Peter sent him.

A few hours later four squad cars pull into Peters driveway and demand that he come out with his hands up. Totally disoriented, Peter demands an explanation. Armed Robbery and Murder were committed in your name tonight at the 7-11.

Would it be fair for Peter to be locked away for life for crimes done in his name? Crimes that he would never have approved? Many things have been done in the name of Christ that directly contradict everything He stood for. Is it fair to condemn Christianity or Jesus Christ because of the things done in his name?

The Search
Open Forum

The Open Forum is a gathering of friends for the purpose of interacting on significant life and God issues. Normally, it takes place in a home and lasts for four weeks. The guests enjoy eating, meeting each other, laughing and sharing their thoughts. It is an authentic, stimulating discussion about basic life issues, not a Bible study, lecture series or theological debate.

The objective is to help our friends examine their philosophy of life. Many people have never carefully evaluated their beliefs, and the Open Forum provides a comfortable environment to do this.

The Open Forum normally begins with a nucleus of people who meet to plan for a series of discussions. This core group then invites a wider network of friends and associates to participate in any or all of the four gatherings.

Search sets up several guidelines to ensure a stimulating dialogue that is comfortable, affirming and challenging. Three promises are reviewed at the beginning of each discussion:

1. The forum is a group discussion, not a debate or a lecture, and no one person or viewpoint will dominate.
2. The discussion is limited to one hour to respect the time of the people who come. Informal conversations often continue afterwards.
3. If and when appropriate, the Bible's perspective on a topic will be offered as one of the options to be considered.

The Open Forum is effective wherever believers have invested in relationships with seekers—including their neighborhoods, small groups and businesses.

Sample Schedule of an Open Forum

	Week 1		Week 2		Week 3	
	Prelim 1	*During the Week...* Generate Invitation List	**Prelim 2**	*During the Week...* Prayer, Invitations and Personal Contact (Additional invitation list)	**Prelim 3**	*During the Week...* Prayer, Invitations and Personal Contact (Additional invitation list)
7:00ish	About an hour • What will happen? • How to invite... • Who to invite... (why will they come?) • Minor details like place, food, and time...		About an hour • Barriers to belief • Open Forum Dynamics (discussion guidelines) • Invitations		About an hour • Basics of Gospel • Open Forum Mechanics (Before, after, and between the meetings.) • Making the most of the Forum	

	Week 4		Week 5		Week 6		Week 7		Week 8
7:00ish	Snacks Name tags	*During the Week...* Prayer & Follow-up	Snacks Name tags	*During the Week...* Prayer & Follow-up	Snacks Name tags	*During the Week...* Prayer & Follow-up	Snacks Name tags	*After the Series...* Prayer and Follow-up	Follow-up Meeting
7:30ish	3 Promises Open Discussion for 59:50		3 Promises Open Discussion for 59:50		3 Promises Open Discussion for 59:50		3 Promises Open Discussion for 59:50		Core group • Evaluation of Forum • Discuss responses of the guests • Plan for further follow-up with the guests
8:30ish	Desserts Conversations Continue...		Desserts Conversations Continue...		Desserts Conversations Continue...		Desserts Conversations Continue...		

One small group's experience with the Open Forum

Nearly everyone at the Thursday night Bible study had mixed feelings about hearing a guest speaker on lifestyle evangelism. They were eager to learn new approaches for communicating their faith. But few had experienced much success in seeing friends come to Christ, and they were apprehensive about discussing the subject.

"Tonight,"the leader, Tom, announced, "I have asked Mike Berry, an attorney here in town, to start off our next few weeks of study on communicating Christ. He has worked with a group called Search and has led a number of Open Forum discussion series. Mike has some very fresh and exciting ideas about sharing our faith."

"The basic philosophy of Search,"Mike began, "is lifestyle evangelism. I understand that this group has talked about lifestyle evangelism before. Tell me what you're thinking."

"Lifestyle evangelism is an exciting concept," Jim volunteered. "I have a fair number of friends who I either know are not believers or else I'm uncertain about their spiritual condition. I really do care deeply that they come to know Jesus Christ and experience what He has done for Mary and me. But we just haven't known how to communicate the message without alienating them."

Brenda nodded in agreement. "I know what you

mean,"she said. "It would be great if my friend Lisa could get involved in an investigative study, but I have a feeling she would be threatened by a Bible study."

A Unique Discussion Series

"You may be right,"said Mike. "Many people find it threatening to attend a Bible study with a room full of strangers. That's where the Search Open Forum fits in perfectly. Let me explain briefly how it works."

"The Open Forum is a series of eight weekly meetings. The first three weeks are what we call preliminary meetings. The next four are discussions to which believers invite their friends and neighbors to openly talk about life and God issues. The eighth meeting is for follow up."

"In the three preliminary meetings,"Mike continued, "a core group of those who have a personal relationship with Christ meet to examine biblical perspectives on communicating their faith.We draw up a guest list of friends and acquaintances we would like to invite to the four discussions and we pray for each aspect of the Open Forum. Then we prepare for the discussions."

"What do you do to prepare?"asked Linda.

"We discuss group dynamics and relational skills,"Mike said. "We also review the message of eternal life and how to communicate it in the context of open discussion."

"Will we ask our friends to make a decision for Christ right at the discussions?"asked Jim.

"Well,"Mike answered, "some guests receive Christ during the course of the four weeks. But others may respond months later as they continue to interact with you on some of the issues raised at the Open Forum"

The Three Phases

"What happens at the Forum discussions" asked Tom.

"There are actually three phases,"Mike explained. "The first phase is a mixer. We want to create a warm, casual atmosphere with plenty of delicious desserts and hors d'oeuvres. Sometimes we have a whole meal. That will be up to the core group, since they provide the food. The idea is to make people comfortable and have a good time in a casual social setting for the first hour or so."

"We can handle that,"group members agreed.

"I'm sure you can,"Mike said. "Now, to carry this non-threatening atmosphere into Phase Two, the discussion or Forum, we have a few ground rules. While we believe strongly that Bible study and corporate prayer are integral to our preliminary meetings, once the Forum starts, we have neither. There will also be no invitations during the discussions."

"The discussion lasts exactly one hour,"continued Mike, "and then we have Phase Three, more informal discussion that continues over dessert. This may last for an hour or longer."

The Three Promises

Now Mike had the group's attention. Their anticipation had given way to curiosity. "What kinds of things are discussed during the four weeks?"asked Mary.

"Before the discussion actually begins,"Mike explained, "the Forum leader makes three promises. Promise number one, 'This is a discussion and not a lecture. Your opinions and questions are essential if this evening is to be profitable and stimulating.'"

"Promise number two, 'This discussion will last for one hour.' And promise number three, 'From time to time, I will give the biblical perspective on the issue under discussion. You may say whatever you like as we discuss these God and life issues. Feel free to disagree. As a matter of fact, the more friendly disagreement, the more stimulating and enjoyable this discussion will be.'"

Getting Things Started

"Getting back to your question, Mary,"Mike said, "there are many proven ways to begin a discussion. After the three promises are given, the leader may simply ask the group, "What would you like to talk about?" or he or she may begin with a controversial quote or question."

"Such as what?"asked Jim.

"For example,"Mike said, "'Is it important to be good?' or, 'What do you think is the origin of religion, man's creativity or the influence of the divine?' Or, the leader may ask questions that typically come up in discussions anyway, such as 'How do you know there is a God?' 'If God is loving why does He allow so much evil and suffering in the world?' 'Isn't religion just a psychological crutch?' 'Is the Bible accurate and reliable?' The leader may allow someone to choose one of these questions or start the discussion in some other innovative way."

"Can you predict how a discussion will go?"asked Brenda.

"Each discussion is unique,"Mike replied, "but I can give you an idea of some typical issues that come up."

A Typical Forum Discussion

"Suppose a question was raised about how good a life one has to live to get to heaven. Chances are someone would say, 'Well, you simply have to do the best you can and try to live a good life.'"

"Someone else might comment, 'I think it's important to live a good life, too, but maybe we should define what 'good' means.' At that point in the discussion there would probably be a number of suggestions on how to define 'good.' After a few minutes, it might become obvious that what is good behavior for one person or society may not be considered good for another."

"Then,"continued Mike, "someone is likely to suggest as a standard for good behavior the Ten Commandments or the golden rule."

"The next thing that usually happens is very interesting. People in the group find it necessary to acknowledge and deal with their inability to measure up to any of those definitions or standards of good. Someone might say, 'I think we have developed a good standard, but my problem is that I don't always measure up to that standard of goodness. Just how good is good enough?'"

"What has been said in the group so far," Mike continued, "is that one must be good to get to heaven, and that true goodness is following the Ten Commandments or obeying the golden rule. If that is true,then we are all in a great deal of trouble since none of us perfectly measures up to these standards."

"Then someone in the group is likely to suggest, 'But surely God knows that we're not perfect. I think that all one needs to do is try his or her best.' There will probably be a chorus of agreement in the room as people see that this is a way out of the dilemma."

"About this time, someone may take the discussion a bit further by asking, 'Is there anyone in this room who does his or her best?' As an Open Forum leader, I have often said something like, 'According to what the group has suggested is necessary to get to heaven, I flunk. I don't always measure up to the definitions of good behavior, I haven't always followed the Ten Commandments, I haven't even always done my best.'"

"Suspense begins to build in the group as people begin to see cracks in their common conceptions about God and how to get to heaven. However, the group is not yet through trying to come up with a man made solution for the sin problem. The next shift in the discussion is often the suggestion that, 'Surely God is a forgiving God and will understand that we cannot be perfect'"

"At this point, the Forum leader may want to introduce the concept of justice. 'What if God is not only loving and compassionate and forgiving but also just and pure and holy? Would He not be violating His own standards of justice if He were to lower them to accept me? Would not God have to lower His standards infinitely to accept even the best one of us here in this room?'"

"By the way,"Mike interjected, "the discussion I have been relating to you in the past couple of minutes may have taken us forty-five or fifty minutes in actual group discussion. I think by now you can see the dynamics of what is taking place in a typical discussion. We allow people to ask their own questions, not ours. We allow them the freedom to express their opinions, whatever they are. We help them to think through the issues out loud and to realize for themselves, often for the first time, some of the serious flaws in their systems of belief."

"It is at this point,"he continued, "while discussing

particular issues, that we have a beautiful opportunity to present Christ's answer to a question. They have thought through the issues and have discovered some of the problems for themselves, and now they are ready to hear the solution."

"Who presents the solution?" Brenda asked.

"This can be done by the Forum leader at some point during the discussion," Mike said, "or it can be done by the Forum leader and the Christians in the core group on an individual basis after the meeting as they talk with their friends–which brings me to the third phase of the forum, the aftermeeting."

The Aftermeeting

"We tend to think of evangelism in terms of a program rather than a process," Mike explained. "In the case of the Open Forum, people may think that evangelism only takes place during the hour discussion. However, we have found that the discussion hour itself serves primarily as a catalyst for further discussion."

"We use the discussion hour to 'stir up the pot' in someone's thinking," he continued, "to get them interested in a particular issue and whet their appetite for more. The aftermeeting provides time to continue the discussion informally, one-on-one over more good food. This aftermeeting is a terrific time for follow up with those who have attended. For an hour or more, friends have the opportunity to listen and clarify. Questions are answered and relationships are built and strengthened."

"What if a friend enjoys the discussions and expresses interest, but isn't ready to make a decision?" asked Tom.

"That frequently happens," Mike said, "and that's why the Open Forum includes an eighth week for follow up."

The Follow Up Meeting

"Some have come to Christ in the time following the actual discussion," continued Mike, "and many others have come to Christ in the weeks and months after the final discussion."

"At the follow up meeting, the core group gathers without their guests to evaluate the Open Forum and the guests' responses. Some may have come to Christ at an aftermeeting, during informal conversation with friends. Many others may come to Christ in the weeks and months after the final discussion."

"If friends seemed receptive to the message of eternal life, the core group may want to plan a small group Bible study, personal meetings, or more social events to keep the discussion alive."

"Now that I have given you some basic information regarding a Search Open Forum, I'd like to try to answer any other questions you may have," said Mike.

Inviting Friends

John had the first question. "This sounds terrific, Mike. I think if I could get them there, my friends would thoroughly enjoy this kind of discussion. But how do you invite someone to a discussion like this? Is the idea to disguise it so they won't realize what it is until they get there?"

"Quite the contrary," said Mike. "One of the best things about this discussion series is that it will sound interesting and appealing to your friends. Try to remember two guidelines for inviting someone. First, avoid any clichés such as, 'Please join us in our Bible study, church group, or religious meeting as we talk about the Lord.' These are not only the kinds of things that turn people off, they are also inaccurate ways to describe what is actually going to take place in these discussions."

"Second, you must be sure to let them know what the evening is really all about. Let me give you an example. John, I'd like you to act as though you are a seeking friend whom I want to invite to the four discussions."

Mike began, "'Some friends of ours have decided to host a series of discussions at their home, John, and we would love to have you and Judy join us. You know, we often have a great time talking about sports or hobbies or the weather, but we don't often talk about some of the most important issues of life. Sarah and I are really looking forward to this opportunity to be in a stimulating discussion with our good friends, and would love for you to join us.'"

"Well, that does sound interesting," said John, "but what kinds of issues will you be discussing?"

"'I have never actually taken part in one of these discussions before, but I've heard that people ask questions like, 'If God really is a loving God, then how come there's so much suffering in the world?' 'Is religion a psychological crutch for the emotionally unstable?' 'What about all the hypocrites in the church?' 'How good is good enough to get to heaven?' The discussions, I am told, cover any number of life and God issues, and we can hardly wait to get involved.'"

"That does sound interesting when you put it that way," John said.

Mike then turned his attention to the rest of the group. "You see, if my friend John came to the Open Forum based on that invitation, there would be no surprises. He would find exactly the kind of discussion I briefly described for him. And since the core group is determined to help people feel comfortable once they are there, you have nothing to lose as far as your relationship with your friend is concerned. In all likelihood, he or she will have a great time and will be quite stimulated by the discussion hour."

Mary asked, "How many people or couples do you need to sponsor an Open Forum?"

"Good question," replied Mike. "While we have held Open Forums with a fairly small number in the core group, we have generally found that it works best if we have twelve to twenty people who will be committed to praying, inviting people, and bringing delicious food."

"That way we are practically assured of having a healthy number of people in attendance. We feel this is very important since the more guests there are, the more comfortable they will feel. It always makes people feel good when they hear someone else asking their kind of questions."

There was now a sense of enthusiasm among the group. "If there are no more questions," Mike said, "let me conclude with some perspective and summary. The Open Forum is like the tip of an iceberg that breaks through the water's surface and can be easily seen. The four-fifths below the surface is the willingness of believers to pray persistently for their friends and neighbors and to spend quality social time with them, deepening those relationships. The Open Forum won't be successful if the prayer and relationships are missing. And, of course, there must be continued contact with your friends after the Open Forum, either for follow up of a new believer or for the continued building of the relationship."

"This has been a most stimulating evening, Mike," said Tom, "and I don't know how to thank you for your time and insights. I, for one, am ready to get moving and get involved in an Open Forum. If the group agrees, we'll get our schedules together and figure out a good night of the week to hold the discussions and check back with you this week."

It was a big step for nearly everyone in the group, but they were united in their agreement.

For the first time, communicating their faith in Christ sounded like a natural part of their lifestyle rather than an awkward appendage. They prayed expectantly together that night in anticipation of what God would do in the lives of their friends, and went home with a new excitement about cultivating relationships

www.ingramcontent.com/pod-product-compliance
Lightning Source LLC
LaVergne TN
LVHW071132160826
845679LV00005B/1255
9798843069247